Practical Crowdfunding How-To-Guide

What You Need To Know To Run An Effective Campaign

Steven Imke

Produced in the United States of America

First Printing, 2016

ISBN-13:978-1534701427
ISBN-10:1534701427

KSI Enterprises
395 Scrub Oak Circle
Monument CO 80132

www.SteveBizBlog.com

About the Author

Steve's first foray into the world of small business came when he was an Invisible Fencing dealer. He operated this business on a part-time basis while remaining employed by a Fortune 500 company called Digital Equipment Corporation (DEC). While the Invisible Fencing business was not very successful for Steve, it was a valuable opportunity for him to learn important lessons about business in a relatively low-risk environment.

After ending his relationship with Invisible Fencing, he worked on a business plan for a new business idea and waited for the right opportunity to present itself. In 1994, DEC fell on hard times. Instead of bemoaning this turbulent economic tide, Steve capitalized on this opportunity. He quit his day job at DEC to found Horizon Interactive, a documentation and training company. In fact, Horizon Interactive became a vendor for DEC.

Over the next few years, Steve and his partners executed the business plan. The business grew to over $3 million in annual sales and opened offices in several states. Horizon Interactive's success drew the attention of Interleaf, a publicly held company out of Massachusetts. In 1999, Interleaf acquired Horizon Interactive.

As part of the acquisition, Steve was offered the position of VP of Operations for their services division. Under his leadership, Interleaf acquired two more businesses like

Horizon Interactive. The company grew the services side of the business from a combined $8 million in revenue to over $32 million in sales during the next two years.

In 2001, Interleaf was acquired by Broadvision, a California company during the height of the dot com era. Broadvision primarily acquired Interleaf for their XML engineers who worked on the product side of the business. Needing to divest himself from the services business, Steve and a former business partner acquired the assets of Interleaf's service business and started IC Interactive. They operated the business for a few more years until they sold it in 2003.

Being a serial entrepreneur, Steve has started and still operates three different businesses. One of his businesses is focused on real estate. The second one is focused on oil and gas. His third business is a company designed to help high net-worth investors understand the ins and outs of investing in oil and gas direct participation programs.

Steve has volunteered his time since 2003 as a mentor for SCORE, a local organization dedicated to helping entrepreneurs. He has acted as their Chapter Chairman for several years. He is also an advisory board member of his local Small Business Development Center (SBDC). In additions to his advisory role, he also acts as a counselor for the SBDC since 2003. In 2012, Steve acted as the interim director of SBDC while they conducted a national search for a permanent director. Currently, Steve is the Entrepreneurship Director at Pikes Peak Community College and writes a daily blog about small businesses.

Steve is a flaming dyslexic, which has its good points and bad points. Growing up, he remembers undergoing a board of education evaluation. When asked to draw a tree, Steve drew a series of concentric rings. When asked about his drawing, he said the rings were what you see when you cut down the tree and look at the stump. These rings tell the entire life story of the tree. The evaluator told his parents he was not normal. He should be more like the other kids and draw the tree from the side view.

However, rather than conform to the crowd, Steve embraced his out-of-the-box thinking as an asset. The upside of being dyslexic is exceptional spatial awareness and problems solving skills. Dyslexics develop these heightened skills since they are forced from an early age to compensate for things they do not do well.

Being a dyslexic in school prevented Steve from becoming a good reader. Even today, spelling and grammar are not his strong suits. Academically, Steve struggled in traditional schools. When he graduated from high school, he knew that a traditional classroom education was not for him so he joined the United States Coast Guard to learn a trade. Graduating near the top of his class in tech school, Steve realized that he learned by doing.

Steve tends to be an overly logical person. He likes to explore, document, and measure nearly every aspect of a project to find out what works and what does not. He has a propensity to focus on understanding why things are the way they are rather than how to duplicate what others have already done. Once Steve obtains a reasonable level of mastery in a specific subject area, he internalizes the knowledge and moves on to his next area of interest.

Everything of substance Steve knows about small business initially began by him reading books, listening to audiobooks, or watching others. He internalizes the salient points, then rolls up his sleeves and puts them into practice in his own business. Once Steve perfects a lesson, he makes it a point to document it and then share it with others. He calls these "Sea Stories," leveraging his old Coast Guard days. In addition to sharing his knowledge, this practice serves to further solidify his learning in his own mind while continuing to grow his knowledge base. In this way, Steve has codified over more than a decade's worth of his small business knowledge in the various books he has written.

This process has served Steve pretty well. By the time he was 42 years old, Steve had reached the point where he no longer needed to work for money. Passing this income milestone has not only allowed him the luxury to spend even more time to ponder and digest life's lessons, but also the freedom to tell it like it is without the fear of losing his job. He proudly wears jeans nearly every day. He also sports facial hair to remind himself and others that being a nonconformist and not subscribing to traditional viewpoints has its merits for entrepreneurs.

Steve constantly reads and listens to non-fiction audiobooks about politics or business related topics. He consumes current events from a huge basket of news sources every day so he can relate their messages in new and innovative ways. After internalizing a message and testing new theories, he shares his new-found wisdom with people willing to listen.

Since 2003, Steve has mentored and counseled thousands of fledgling entrepreneurs through his volunteer efforts with SCORE and SBDC. He has volunteered his expertise to help organizations like ARC, a program which helps individuals with developmental disabilities.

As cliché as it may sound, Steve is at the point in his life where it is all about using his skills and knowledge to help others to succeed. Steve never expects anything in return, but simply enjoys the appreciation he receives from the people he has helped and lives vicariously through their success. For Steve, sharing his knowledge is akin to the feeling a billionaire might have handing out $100 bills to random strangers on the street. He knows that by sharing some of the wisdom he has accumulated with clients, he can often make a positive difference in their lives. Steve is not particularly religious so helping entrepreneurs is his way of giving back and making a significant impact on the world around him.

Table of Contents

Part 1: Crowdfunding Facts and Considerations

Crowdfunding 101

Generally speaking, crowdfunding is divided into creative campaigns, reward-based campaigns, and equity campaigns. In creative campaigns, such as a Michael Moore movie, the backers support the message or the "art" and make donations to help promote the cause. Creative campaigns have been around forever, however reward-based and equity campaigns are relatively new. In reward-based campaigns, the business provides actual rewards for the contributions made by backers. While in equity campaigns, the founders give away micro equity positions to backers.

Before crowdfunding, investments in a business was limited to the founder, friends, family, and accredited investors. Title II and Title III of the JOBS bill changed all that. Under the JOBS bill, founders can solicit strangers to invest in their business and raise money in new ways giving birth to reward-based and equity crowdfunding.

So, why doesn't every founder use crowdfunding to raise money?. The answer lies in the fact that many campaigns simply fail. To be more specific, 60% of creative/reward-based campaigns and 80% of equity campaigns fail. Why do they fail to meet their funding goals? The reason is that the people running the campaign are using traditional marketing rules and crowdfunding does not respond well to traditional marketing. Crowdfunding is not traditional fundraising and requires businesses to use a completely different set of marketing concepts.

The big difference is that crowdfunding is much more personal and less about business. Investing in a crowdfunding campaign is like participating in a reality show except instead of just watching, the backers are participants.

Backers of crowdfunding campaigns are not savvy businessmen who are only driven by numbers. Rather, they are regular hardworking people that are seeking a social connection to something that is lacking in their busy work filled lives. They desire to be part of something bigger than themselves. Therefore, a successful crowdfunding campaign must be marketed with a more personal prospective than a business one.

Backers want to live vicariously through the project they invest in. That's why it is important to convey your personal journey to them so they can feel more connected and a part of your vision. Relating your project as a story and making it personal will help make an impact on your potential crowdfunding backers.

When it comes to using a platform like Kickstarter or Indiegogo, the typical platform costs are about 5% for commission and a 3% processing fee similar to a credit card transaction fee. To illustrate, a business that raises $10K only nets $9.2K in funding proceeds. It should also be noted that most creative/reward-based campaigns raise less than $10K, however some equity campaigns have raise millions. Generally speaking, it is better to host multiple campaigns based on program milestones. For instance, you could hold one campaign to raise money to develop a minimally viable product (MVP) and then another campaign to get the product into production, etc.

The actual campaign window where you are accepting money should be about 30-45 days long. They need to be short enough to create a sense of urgency yet long enough to reach your goal amount.

While there is a huge amount of work to do before you launch your campaign, it is best to try and schedule the campaign around a major event, such as a conference or an expo. This will help promote your campaign at the event and build need buzz. These campaigns work best if you have a prototype or something concrete to leverage support from the industry people who attend the event.

When it comes to rewards, be sure to spell out the reward time frames. While some rewards, such as a t-shirt, can be shipped close to the end date of the campaign, other rewards, such as the V1.0 version of the product, will take much longer to deliver. When it comes to delivery dates, it is better to under-promise and over-deliver.

If, however, you suspect it will take longer to deliver rewards than you quoted, it is best to communicate the news to your backers as soon as possible. Backers tend to invest in several programs. If you start missing deadlines, the community you worked so hard to build will abandon you making it much harder to raise more money in the future.

Is crowdfunding an option for your next raise?

15 Popular Crowdfunding Platforms

There are a wide array of crowdfunding platforms, each with its own unique spin on raising funds. Some platforms support charitable or creative campaigns, others reward-based campaigns, while still others support equity-based campaigns. Some are for accredited investors only while some are open to all types of investors. Some are designed to help raise funds for product development while others are looking for donations to help an individual or family deal with personal needs. While some are designed to help charities raise money. The following list should help you make some sense out of which platforms are best suited for your crowdfunding needs:

- **Kickstarter** is the largest platform with over 13 million visitors a month. It is a good platform to host product and event campaigns, but not social causes.
- **Indiegogo** has upwards of 9 million visitors a month and is similar to Kickstarter. Here you can raise funds for any legal project. It is a good platform for not only raising funds from domestic sources, but international ones as well.
- **RocketHub** is the next most popular platform and is known for its support system "Success School." It offers many funding models, including ones where you get to keep pledges even is you never meet your funding goals at the

end of the campaign. Since they partner with A&E, business owners have the chance of being featured on TV and on the A&E website.

- **Crowdrise** is similar to RocketHub in that it has flexible funding models where you can keep pledges even if your goals are not met. It is one of the biggest platforms to raise money for social causes.
- **Fundable** is one of the few platforms that offers both equity-based and reward-based crowdfunding. What makes it unique is that it does not work on a commission based on the amount of money raised. This quality makes it attractive for large projects.
- **AngelList** is a platform for start-ups to meet accredited investors and is geared for equity-based campaigns only.
- **SeedInvest** is a platform like AngelList that enables accredited investors to invest in start-ups.
- **CircleUp** is an equity only platform that connects accredited investors, innovative consumers, and retail companies. Companies must have existing revenue in excess of $500K to be listed. Funding can be through convertible debt or equity.
- **WeFunder** is another equity-based crowdfunding platform for accredited investors only, but allows for pledges as small as $100.

- **GoFundMe** is a popular platform for personal fundraising causes (e.g., covering medical expenses), but also for a select group of charities. They also support reward-based all-or-nothing campaigns similar to Kickstarter.
- **YouCaring** is another platform for charitable and personal causes with specific categories for medical, funeral, tuition, adoption, faith-based, pet expenses, and community causes.
- **GiveForward** is a donation-based platform with specific categories for medical bills, veterinarian bills, and funeral expenses.
- **Patreon** is a platform for fans to support their favorite creative projects such as music or video projects on a more ongoing basis.
- **AlumniFinder** is a relatively new platform to fund creative and innovative projects within a university community.
- **CauseVox** is a platform tool for developers to develop their own website for peer to peer fundraising campaigns.

Which crowdfunding platform is right for your next fundraising campaign?

The Hidden Value of Crowdfunding

Traditionally, entrepreneurs had 2 options to raise funds to start their business. They could either get a loan or give away ownership to investors. Because of the risk involved in the early stages of a small business, founders had to give up large blocks of equity to entice an early stage equity investor. On the other hand, having to make interest and principle payments for debt financing can, at best, slow growth or even cripple a company during it's fragile early stages. Enter crowd funding, a viable option to preserve equity and eliminate the need for debt.

In a real estate deal a few years ago, a builder I know needed to raise capital to build a new residential tower in downtown Denver. With a mock-up of the finished building, some computer generated images, and some floor plan layouts, he pre-sold many of the units at a discount to come up with the seed money he needed to get the project off the ground. Crowdfunding shares many similarities to the strategy used by the builder to raise capital and validate the concept.

In many cases, a product-based crowdfunding campaign allows people to pre-order the product before anyone else.

This campaign accomplishes several vital steps for a company still in its early stages.

1. It provides the company with the capital it needs to build the first wave of products without either giving away equity, or pay back principle, or pay the lender interest. These benefits occur when equity is most under valued and capital preservation is most needed.
2. It validates the hypothesis that consumers are willing to exchange cash for the product. Proving the value of the product is a major tenet of the business model canvas and for business that employ the lean start-up methodology.
3. It can raise to the surface demand for new and innovative products that might be hidden without a large number of investors actually seeing the product.
4. It attracts early adopters who become social activists, evangelizing the product to their networks and raising product awareness.
5. Tiered raises create excitement. Excitement can create a valuable feedback loop to further product improvement by exposing the product to early adopters, the people who are most likely to provide feedback.
6. It provides funding for a particular product and not the company. It is like a direct investment in a single oil well rather than buying the diversified portfolio of an oil company, such as Exxon.

In addition to pre-order campaigns, some crowdfunding campaigns, known as equity-based campaigns, allow for micro ownership of an early stage company. This creates a whole new class of investors who can buy into companies before they become large and go public.

Before equity-based crowdfunding, only accredited investors (investors with more than a million dollars in net-worth or investors that earn over two hundred thousand per year in wages) could get involved with ground floor investments.

Prior to crowdfunding, companies who tried to raise money from unaccredited investors would run afoul with the Securities and Exchange Commission (SEC).

Crowdfindinng allows small investment levels that bypasses SEC oversight, opening the opportunity for micro investors wanting to buy into early stage companies. These micro investors hope these businesses will grow substantially. They hope that these businesses will then give them a significant return on their investment when the company experiences a exit event such as being acquired or going public.

Before crowdfunding, even accredited investors would have to either invest large sums of money in only a few companies, which is very risky since there is limited diversity in invested capital, or find a venture capital fund to invest in and lose ultimate control over the specific investment allocations in new companies. With crowdfunding, a small time investor with only a few thousands dollars can invest in dozens of hand picked companies and achieve investment diversification, a domain only previously available to venture capital principle investors.

Setting up a crowdfunding campaign generally requires a good video demonstration of a sexy new product. Need a little help getting your idea from conception to a point where you are ready to begin a crowdfunding campaign? No problem! Companies, such as Quirky can help get you there in exchange for micro equity stakes.

However, the funding of your venture may be the easy part. The real work comes when the new company or product gets funded. Now the owners must produce the product. To do that, they must now manage a long supply chain and learn to run a real business.

Are you considering crowdfunding to your next product?

Some Equity-Based Crowdfunding Statistics

CrowdCube is the largest equity-based crowdfunding platform in the United Kingdom. Since its founding in 2008, it has facilitated more than $60 million in transactions to date. Combined, those transactions have involved nearly 88,000 investors and over 140 successfully funded ventures.

The average individual equity-based investment was approximately $4,000, although investments ranged from as little as $15 to as large as $400,000.

Based on their statistics, the average successful venture attracts 104 equity-based investors and approximately $370,000 in capital raised. That said, only about 1 in 4 were successful in reaching their funding goal.

Is equity-based crowdfunding for you?

Information Asymmetry in Equity Crowdfunding

Start-up investment is characterized by a high degree of information asymmetry between the entrepreneur and the investors. To obtain a positive return, investors need to accurately assess both the qualifications and ability of an entrepreneur. They also need to accurately assess the potential of the entrepreneur's idea.

Traditional institutional investors are professionals who have the expertise and experience necessary to evaluate potential investment opportunities. These institutional investors frequently take a trip to visit the founder and his team to get a physical demo of the product.

In contrast, crowdfunders are typically known as retail investors. They have relatively limited experience or resources to support their evaluation of new ventures. Making matters worse, the investors are often geographically separated and rarely, if ever, meet the founder or get their hands on a demonstration to make their evaluation. Therefore, evaluating your investment in an equity-based crowdfunding project is a much greater challenge.

How can you overcome the information asymmetry associated with equity crowdfunding?

Taxes and Crowdfunding

While crowdfunding is becoming more and more common, tax support and guidance for the campaign creators continue to remain unclear on many points. At a minimum, the tax treatment of funds generated through crowdfunding depends on whether the campaign is reward-based, donation-based, or equity-based. Moreover, if it is reward-based, the value of any reward offered also becomes a factor, especially when the value of the reward, such as product naming rights, is difficult to determine.

Pledges received from donation-based crowdfunding are likely to be considered as nontaxable gifts while equity-based crowdfunding is more likely to be consider paid-in capital. Neither of which are generally subject to income tax.

However, it should be noted that the money you raise through contributions from backers for reward-based campaigns are considered revenue for the business by the IRS and are subject to income taxes. Also, the money raised may be subjected to state excise, sales, and/or business and occupation tax in some states. Therefore, you must track all your campaign expenses carefully to reduce your tax burden, just as you would with any business.

Moreover, if the campaign raises money in one tax year and incurs some or all of the expense of fulfilling the campaign's rewards in the subsequent tax year, the company may experience tax induced cash flow issues. As a result, it is always a good idea to consult your CPA to discuss your tax related issues prior to undertaking any crowdfunding campaign.

How will income taxes affect your crowdfunding campaign?

Part 2: The Process

Crowdfunding Process Overview

So, you have a gem of an idea and want to get it off the ground. The first question is how much will it cost and can you come up with the money. We know that going to a lending institution like a bank to secure a business loan is an unlikely option and attracting a bunch of investors other than family members is a stretch. However, conducting a crowdfunding campaign to raise seed money and prove that the market will embrace and pay money for your idea sounds appealing.

The first step, regardless of which options you decided to ultimately take, is to figure out just how much funding you will need to raise. Tools like our Startup worksheet and Cash Flow statement that can be found on the resources tab of my blog can give you a good start at understanding your financing requirements. However, most successful businesses begin with some kind of plan.

As with most businesses, it is best to shape your business idea with the Business Model Canvas and then use the data to write a business plan. At the end of the planning process, you will need to determine how to fund your idea.

If crowdfunding is the right way for you to raise money, it is not a as simple as launching a campaign and waiting for the money to roll in. A successful campaign takes work.

You do not want to become one of the failed statistics after all. In fact, there are eleven distinctly different steps to a successful crowdfunding campaign:

1. Platform Research
2. Campaign Research
3. Campaign Support
4. Going Social
5. Campaign Influencers
6. Campaign Blog
7. Community Building
8. Design Rewards
9. Campaign Write-up
10. Campaign Execution
11. Campaign Follow-up

Is crowdfunding an option for your next raise?

Platform Research

When it comes to campaign research, it is all about researching what projects work best on each platform to determine which is the best platform to launch your campaign.

In most cases, platform research should take you about a week or so to do effectively. Using the Google search engine is an effective way to start your research. This approach helps you find campaigns similar to the one you intend to launch.

First, try to Google a "platform" followed by the "your product idea." For example, say you have an idea for a new Mini Drone product. You might enter "KickStarter Mini

Drone" to get a list of similar campaigns to start your research.

Another Google search may be to enter simply "Crowdfunding Mini Drone."

Once you locate similar products search the campaign for the following information:

- What was their initial fundraising target goal?
- How much were they able to raise?
- How many backers did they have?
- What were the pledge amounts?
- What rewards did they offer?
- What was their video message like?
- How did they connect with the backer's emotions?
- What was the length of their campaign?
- What was the timeline to deliver their rewards?
- Click on the comments section to see what was said about the campaign.
- Look at their website or blog. What you can learn from them?

What does your proposed campaign have in common with other campaigns?

How is it different?

What can you use from your research to make your campaign better?

Campaign Research

After you complete your platform research, the next step is for you to locate and reach out to each of the campaign owners or founders. Ask them if they would be willing to discuss their campaign experience. In most cases, campaign research should take you about another week or so to do effectively.

You may want to begin by sending the campaign owners a brief introduction email, saying you saw their campaign and were impressed. Add that you are thinking about launching a similar campaign. Many platforms include a link for you to contact the owner or founder. Ask if they can spare a few minutes for you to pick their brain about their experience.

If they agree to speak to you, here is a list of information you should try to glean from the discussion:

- Is there any topic specific advice they could share?
- Did they find any social group (e.g., LinkedIn or Facebook) that yielded good interest from members?
- Did they use any online forums or websites that proved successful?
- How about blogs or bloggers that were receptive to guest posts?
- Ask them for a list of journals or publications that were interested in hearing about their campaign.
- What was their biggest challenge?
- If they used Kickstarter or another platform with built-in analytics, see if they are willing to share their campaign analytics with you so you can see who visited the campaign in detail. You will want to see where they came from, what page they sat on, how long they sat on it, when they donated, and how they backed the project.
- If they had to do it all over again, what would they have done differently?
- Finally, see if they will provide you the list of their backers.

As a follow-up, you can enter the campaign name into a Google search engine to find:

- A list of activities they used to promote their campaign
- Posts they used to promote campaign
- The websites they used to promote their campaign

To learn what was said on Twitter about their campaign, you can use the twitter advances search feature to see tweets that discussed their campaign.

What did you learn from talking to similar campaign owners and founders to help you make your upcoming campaign better?

Campaign Support

Campaign support is about introducing your campaign to a list of people that might be interested in not only supporting you, but in helping you throughout the process. In most cases, campaign support should take you about 2 weeks or so to do effectively. At this point, your making people aware of the fact you will be launching a campaign in the near future. Your goal is not only to ask them for advice to help them feel engaged with your campaign, but also to get them to agree to share your campaign communications and blog posts once you begin developing them.

During campaign outreach, your goal is to bring people into the campaign and create a sense of community.

Specifically, you will want to reach out either in person or by phone to your friends and family to discuss your campaign idea and solicit their advice, support, and involvement. When you find an eager party, see if they will be able to help with specific efforts such as writing and sending emails to potential backers, writing posts for the campaign blog, or answering questions about the campaign with potential backers. There is so much work associated with running a campaign that having a team to help you will improve your ability to wage a successful campaign.

Once you have solicited support from your friends and family, it is time to reach out to the backers of similar campaigns. This is the list that you got from other campaign owners in the campaign research step. Contact the backers and say that you see that they have backed similar campaigns. Tell them that you would like their feedback on your upcoming campaign. Now is NOT the time to ask them to pledge their support.

Look at forums for crowdfunding in general and by category to locate potential backers. Use Google to help search for forum names. For example, if you are selling a water bottle for runners, search "forum running." Go to the forum and introduce yourself. Offer some valuable comments. Perhaps you can write a comment indicating the need to think more about the need for proper hydration during a race. Answer other posts and float the idea that you are thinking about a campaign for a new hydration device for runners and want feedback.

Have you gathered enough support and lined up enough help to make your campaign a success?

Going Social

The next phase is focused on social shares. In most cases, the going social phase should take you about a week or so to do effectively.

Developing a campaign Facebook page should be step one. Once your campaign Facebook fan page is complete, you should reach out to the other campaign owners you spoke to a few weeks earlier and ask them to tweet or share your campaign Facebook page through their social network. It is always a good practice to ask them if you can help them in any way since they have been so helpful to you. That way it never appears like your relationship with them is only a one way street.

Utilize Facebook group pages. Search for an affinity with the topic of your campaign. Engage with the groups to build trust by getting involved in community discussions. Search Twitter for hashtags. I find Hashtagify and RiteTag to be particularly helpful in identifying popular hash tags.

Another valuable way to locate active twitter shares for a similar campaign is to use Twitter's advanced search function. In addition to Facebook and Twitter, you may also want to search Pinterest to find related boards.

Do you have a plan to use social media to extend your crowdfunding campaign reach?

Campaign Influencers

The next phase is focused on finding and engaging journals, publications, bloggers, and any other influencers that cover your area. In most cases, finding and reaching out to campaign influencers should take you about a week or so to do effectively. However, before contacting influencers, create a clear story idea that their readers will want to hear about. Perhaps you can tie your campaign to an upcoming event they are reporting on. When it comes to working with journals, publications, and blogs, remember that lead times may be long so it is best to reach out to them early.

A friend of mine, Drew Johnson, ran a successful reward-based crowdfunding campaign for TechWears. He said that he underestimated the lead time of journalists and bloggers. Drew spent a lot of time courting journalists and bloggers prior to his campaign but underestimating lead times produced articles that did not coincide with his campaign window. Therefore, these outlets never achieved the desired effect of boosting campaign awareness when people could still make pledges. In fact, according to Drew, most of the stories appeared after his campaign was over, doing him little good with respect to this campaign's funding goal.

Moreover, he stated that some of the journalists and bloggers only became aware of him after he launched his campaign, which didn't allow them time to produce the article to bring awareness to his campaign. When asked what advice he would share, he stressed trying to find the journalists, bloggers, and publishers early enough in the process so that their articles effectively create precampaign buzz or directly support the campaign fund raising efforts.

To help locate reporters, you can use the HARO website, which is an acronym for "Help A Reporter Out". This website connects you to reporters with information sources. Other sites to help locate reporters are:

- PressRush
- ProfNet
- SourceBottle

Once you have located all of the influencers in your campaign area, you need to make a special effort to personally engage with the most influential of them. Since engaging the right influencers can make or break your campaign, ask your support group to do other campaign outreach activities while you focus on the most influential contacts.

One way to compare the influence of a blog or person's website is to add either the "Alexa" and/or "Complete" browser extensions to your favorite browser. These extensions measure the popularity of sites. I personally use Alexa. When I go to a particular blog or website, I click the "Alexa" extension and look at their global and US traffic ranking numbers. The lower the number the better their rank. I also look to see if the site is trending up or down in its influence. Additionally I often search the site's analytics for more details on their traffic.

You should also go to their Facebook, LinkedIn, and Twitter pages to see how many followers they have.

A way to find even more influencers is to search your topic area in Google and document the top 10 sites or so. You can then use a tool like "moz open site explorer" to do a deep dive into each site. Incidentally, you can get a free 30-day trial, which will be more than enough time for you to do your research.

Enter each of your top 10 URLs. For each search, scroll down to Inbound Links and filter the results by their domain authority (DA). Copy the top 20 or so URLs, leaving you with about 200 URL in total to research. Visit each site and find the author's email or other contact info. Reach out to them to see if they would be interested in doing a piece about your campaign.

Do you have a plan to locate and engage journalists, bloggers, and other publications to extend your crowdfunding campaign's reach even more?

Campaign Blog

Build and maintain your campaign blog in conjunction with community building. Community building is discussed as part of the next step. These steps are conducted simultaneously. When combined, they are the most time consuming portion of the entire crowdfunding campaign. In most cases, these steps will take you about 9 weeks or so to do effectively.

One of the most common ways to build a community is through the use of a campaign blog. This is why we are focusing on this topic as its own step.

When it comes to blog content, it is most effective to locate a few experts that are already part of your network and sent them an email with a few questions you would like them to reply to. When they reply to your email, take your questions and their answers and reformat the email into an interview post for your blog.

In addition to using this interview technique for folks already in your network, try reaching out to authors that have recently published a book on a similar topic and conduct an interview with them too. Since authors are eager to promote their new book, many will be surprisingly receptive to your offer since your post will also be a plug for their book.

You may also choose to do a phone interview to capture the information. When it comes to phone or in-person interviewed, I suggest that you format the information and then ask the interviewee to review the final post to make sure that you captured their information correctly. Since the process of distilling a phone or in-person interview into text allows you to have some creative license regarding the message, all too often key concepts can be misinterpreted.

One of the things that bugs me the most with journalists is that most journalists never ask for a review of their story. They just print their interpretation of the interview. When I was a technical writer, all the content is reviewed and approved by the subject matter experts before it is disseminated. I think that journalists should extend this same courtesy to all interviewees. However, this has not been my experience in journalism. Whenever I read a story that a reporter wrote after I gave them an interview, it almost always contained misinformation. In the end, I often resent the journalist for publishing incomplete or inaccurate information. In summary, treat the interview process like you are a technical writer and not a journalist.

Another effective technique to capture blog content is to use Skype to make the phone call and record it. I use a free tool called MP3 Skype Recorder to record the interview and I use a relatively cheap snowball microphone that I plug into my PC. I make the call via Skype and activate the recorder software. What I like about this solution is that it automatically switches between the caller and you so there is no need to buy a mixing board. You can hear the other party through the PC speakers as if they were physically sitting next to you. You can then save the recording and treat it like a podcast.

You can even edit it with another free tool I use called Audacity. If you want to turn the recording into text, you have the option of sending the MP3 file to a transcription service for a small fee. However for a free option you can play the audio while running the free version of the Dragon Speech to Text app that runs on the iPad. Then all you have to do is add who is speaking to the resulting text file and publish it on your blog.

Keeping up with the blog content is a great job for one of the helpers you enlisted earlier.

Do you have a strategy to develop and maintain a campaign blog as part of your community building activities?

Community Building

Now is the time to send the influencers on your list an email and asked them for advice about your campaign. Be sure to mention that you read their post/article/book. If you mention that you enjoyed reading it, you will increase the likelihood they will reply to your request.

Prioritize your list of influencers and focus on sites and people that are the most active. Read and share information in your topic area to build trust with them before also asking them to support your campaign. Even if you do all the right things, expect about a 10% return rate on your cold contacts. However, with a few good social shares, some campaigns have been able to boost their return rates to 15-20%.

Start sending out emails to your list as you count down to the launch to build momentum. Now is the time to try to get committed backer support prior to your launch date. If necessary, make their pledge contingent on reaching a specific funding level. For example, you might say, "Can I count on you to support us at the platinum level if we raise 20% percent of our goal?" If they are not receptive, ask, "How about supporting us at the gold level?" If necessary, go all the way and ask, "Will you at least support us at the $10 High-Five level?" If you don't ask, most people will not pledge because this is the point in the campaign where you begin to ask for their pledges. Based on successful campaigns, your goal should be to get about 20% of your target amount in pre-launch pledges from your network.

Another effective way to build a community is to have a launch party. The best launch parties build enthusiasm for the campaign and have a creative twist to make them memorable. Perhaps you can buy a canvas and some paint from an art supply company and encourage everyone at the launch party to contribute to a painting you will post on the blog and giver away as a reward after the campaign. Don't be afraid to be creative and don't forget to ask for pledges at the launch party.

Your list of committed backers is different from the ideal backer since your committed backers at this point likely include family and friends. Drew Johnson, a colleague of mine that ran a successful reward-based crowdfunding campaign for TechWears shared the following advice. If he had it all to go over again, he would have scrubbed his look-a-like list when he used a Facebook ad campaign to find backers.

Drew had collected a list of about 500 people who signed up at his various demos and craft fairs where he demonstrated and sold his unique TechWears products. His initial thinking was that since the 500 on his list stopped by his booth, engaged with him in a discussion about his product, and were willing to sign-up for his mailing list that they were all potential backers. Unfortunately, many on the list were "tire kickers" who signed his list more out of politeness rather than genuine interest. When he used his list in a Facebook look-a-like ad campaign, the demographic he targeted was not the audience that was actually looking to buy geek-wear as he calls it. In the end, it cost him more money and did not get him the conversion rate he was hoping for from the ad campaign. Therefore, if you plan to use a Facebook ad campaign and use look-a-like list, you should scrub your list to remove those people not likely to be your ideal backer.

What are your plans for building a community for your next campaign?

Design Rewards

If you are doing a reward-based campaign, one of your tasks is to come up with your reward levels. Equity-based and donation/charity-based campaigns generally do not offer any rewards to backers for their contributions other than ownership or listing the backers contribution level on the campaign pages. Your research from similar campaigns should give you a pretty good idea of the different types of rewards and the popularity of those rewards.

Most campaigns have a "high-five" or similar entry support level that is in the $1-$10 range. As you move up the levels, most rewards are commutative. The average campaigns have between 9 and 12 levels. Below are some examples.

- $10 pledge gets you a personal email or name listed on our website.
- $10 to $50 gets you a personal message plus a logo embossed rubber wristband.
- $50 to $100 gets you the above rewards plus handmade tile for your office.
- $100 to $200 gets you the above plus a personalized brick with your name in front of our offices.
- Etc.

Below are some other reward ideas:

- T-shirt or wristband with brand logo
- Buttons
- Creative naming rights
- Character name in a story if you are writing a book
- Signed picture of our staff
- Signed memorabilia like copies of patent application or engineering drawings

With all rewards, it is a good idea to add a sense of urgency by either limiting the number of rewards at a specific level or limiting the time that a specific level will be available.

What are the reward levels you will use for your next reward-based campaign?

Campaign Write-up

With all the per-work you have done to this point, designing and writing up the campaign will on the platform you chose should take you no more than 1 week in most cases. When it comes to the actual elements within your page design, the best campaigns have the following elements:

- **Title** – The best title is "project name: tagline." For example, "Pogo: Your Personal Robot."
- **Video** – The title should be followed by a short video. According to Kickstarter, campaigns with a video are 15% more likely to get funded than campaigns without a video. If you use a video, you should be featured in it someplace since the

campaign is selling you. Because of it importance in converting visitors into donors you may want to consider hiring a professional to help you do your video.

- **Pitch** – The video is followed by a pitch message that is about 2 paragraphs in length. The pitch should not take any more than 30 seconds to read. Most visitors will only get to this point so be sure to make your pitch relateable. Put yourself in the cause's shoes. The copy you write must create a sense of urgency to encourage the backer to pledge now. The pitch should create a "wow tell me more" moment in the reader so they continue reading. Finally, the pitch should include a request for a pledge as well as a request to become part of your team.

- **Image** – Follow the pitch with an image. Like with the video, you may want to hire a professional photographer that is skilled in capturing emotions. Short of coming up with an original photo, you can use stock photo sites. I like sites such as Flickr.com that contain free photos that you might be able to use for your campaign. If you use Flickr, you can click "Explore," go to "The Commons," and use key words to search for images that you can use for free. I also like to use Google Advanced Image Search https://www.google.com/advanced_image_search tool. To avoid copyright issues, use "usage rights" to filter images you can use.

- **Full Description** – Follow the image with the full description. Too many campaigns include lots of text which is boring. When it comes to appealing to the senses of backers, use images, videos, and even audio in your descriptions to keep your visitors engaged. Audio is a great way to capture testimonials and make your appeal for their support. Once created, the pictures, video, and audio can be used and reused throughout your campaign in emails, blog, and social media.

  In the description, make your visitors understand that backing your campaign is about being part of something bigger than themselves. If you are doing an equity financing campaign, a strong draw to get them to be investors is to stress the fact that they can be part of the business before it is publicly available. In the description, include links to websites or blogs. Include social share buttons so they can promote your campaign to their circles.
- **Budget** – Include an itemized budget at a high level to prove you have thought things through.
- **Time** – Include a timeline for the campaign. Be sure to include all your pre-launch activities and schedule for rewards. When it comes to your timeline and schedules, it is best to add additional time here. It is always better to under-promise and over-deliver than to over-promise and under-deliver.
- **Team** – Include a thumbnail image and brief bio of all key team members.

When you have created your first draft of the campaign, wait a day or two and revise the copy. Then, when the day arrives, submit your campaign page to the platform for review.

Another lesson Drew Johnson shared with me about his TechWares campaign on KickStarter.com was that when it is important to launch at a specific date and time, be sure to know how the campaign start time is established. Drew made the assumption that he would submit his campaign, get approval, and then be given the opportunity to pick a precise launch date and time. What happened was he submitted his campaign for approval 2-days prior to his ideal launch day and time because he had assumed that it could take as much as 48 hours to get a campaign approved according to the platforms submissions directions. To his horror, the campaign went live nearly two days earlier than he planned, throwing his entire launch schedule into chaos.

Do you have a page created for your campaign?

Campaign Execution

Most campaigns run 4 to 6 weeks, long enough to gain enough traction, but short enough to maintain a sense of urgency. Most campaigns see a flurry of support at the start as the backers and influencers you reached out to during the outreach phase make their pledges. Also, there typically is a flurry of support near the end of campaign window as the pledge window's closure creates a sense of urgency.

When it comes to planning your launch, make sure that the start or end dates do not fall on holidays or in the middle of the night or you may miss your most productive pledge activity windows. If possible, consider planning the campaign around a conference or event you can go to with a prototype to build awareness about your product and campaign.

If your campaign window includes a conference or event, be sure everything for your campaign is mobile friendly. With smart phones and tablets, the people you speak to at an event can be encouraged to pledge right there at the conference or event. Perhaps by pledging at the event they can even receive a special gift or recognition for doing so. Make sure that the backers you spoke to in the pre-launch stages know how important it is to pledge on the first day so your campaign has a good chance of getting a featured position by showing campaign traction early on.

It is best to make a schedule ahead of time that you will follow throughout the campaign to keep up awareness and momentum.

When you get money from a backer:
- Use an auto responder to thank them and remind them of the importance of their contribution to the success of the effort.
- Call them the next day to thank them personally. It is not about the amount of the contribution as much as it is about community building.
- After a few days, send them another email and ask if they could forward the campaign information to 3 friends or post your campaign on their social media. If they refuse or simply do not follow through, don't stop requesting their help. Studies have shown that after a rejection, the guilt of the rejection makes

them more likely to grant a follow-up request. In any communication with backers at any level, be sure to make them feel included by referring to it as "our" project. After they pledge, it is not over. They can still help. Continue to express messages that they are part of something bigger.

- Recognize their contribution on your social media, blog, and campaign to make them feel pride. Think about having a "biggest backer" or "backers of the day" message to encourage competition among backers and perhaps lead to multiple rounds of support from backers.

Be sure to include links to your campaign in all emails. You may also want to make several Webcam videos interlaced with other campaign video, pictures, and audio that you can post on your social media platforms.

It is not uncommon for support to drop in the middle of the campaign window. Be sure to keep up momentum by sending updates on funding milestones as they are reached. For example, send out a message when you reach progressive funding milestones (e.g., 20%, 30%, 40% of your goal).

Also be sure to send news, development updates, feedback, testimonials, and when you get support from media or bloggers. Don't forget to mention non-monitory supporters in your communications too. As you reach the end of your campaign, contact your backers and offer special add-on rewards. Try to get a matching gift from an earlier backer or agreement to match other contributions.

How do you plan to keep up the momentum during your campaign?

Campaign Follow-up

Assuming you have met your funding goals, now the work really begins. However, be sure to thank your backers even if your funding goals are not met. Remember it is about community and you may need them in the future.

If you ran a reward-based campaign, you made many reward promises. You should be aware that if you do not make good on your rewards, you may be subject to legal liability.

You will want to continue to use the blog and periodic emails to provide updates and document your post-campaign progress. Be sure to include updates on reward distributions. If you are going to miss a deadline for a reward, share this with your backers before the deadline.

Some campaigns get funded for way more than their goal and reward fulfillment becomes far more complex logistically than planned. For example, you may have thought that you could source, pack, and ship all rewards yourself. However, if you exceed your goals, you will need to hire and train someone to help you, which takes time and costs money.

How do you plan to follow up with your backers once the campaign is over?

www.ingramcontent.com/pod-product-compliance
Lightning Source LLC
Chambersburg PA
CBHW070400190526
45169CB00003B/1051